Grand Army of the Republic

Services for the Use of the Grand Army of the Republic

Grand Army of the Republic

Services for the Use of the Grand Army of the Republic

ISBN/EAN: 9783337220853

Printed in Europe, USA, Canada, Australia, Japan

Cover: Foto ©Andreas Hilbeck / pixelio.de

More available books at **www.hansebooks.com**

FOR THE USE OF THE

GRAND ARMY OF THE REPUBLIC.

·•·

HEADQUARTERS GRAND ARMY OF THE REPUBLIC,
PHILADELPHIA, PA.

April, 1884.

SERVICES.

FOR THE

OBSERVANCE OF MEMORIAL DAY.

IT IS SWEET AND HONORABLE TO DIE FOR ONE'S
COUNTRY.—*Horace*.

SERVICES FOR MEMORIAL DAY.

[THE Post will assemble, at the order of the Post Commander, in the Post Hall (or elsewhere), all comrades in uniform. The officers (if in the Post Hall) will take their usual stations.]

COMMANDER.—Sergeant-Major (*he rises and salutes, the Commander returning salute*), you will prepare for parade. (*The Sergeant-Major will then form the Post in line, two ranks.*)

SERGEANT-MAJOR.—Commander, the Post is formed.

COMMANDER.—Officer of the Day, you will ascertain if all in the ranks are comrades of the G. A. R.

OFFICER OF THE DAY.—All in the ranks are comrades of the G. A. R.

COMMANDER.—Adjutant, you will present the officers. (*The Adjutant will command, "Officers to the front and centre." Will place himself three paces in front and opposite centre of the line, the remaining officers will form on the right and left of the Adjutant, facing the P. C., as follows: S. V. C., Surgeon, Chaplain, Adjutant, O. D., Q. M., O. G., J. V. C.*)

ADJUTANT.—OFFICERS, *Present Arms.*

COMMANDER.—(*Unless he has special orders for officers, will say:*) Officers, to your stations. (*Officers will take their places in line, Chaplain one pace to left and front of the Commander, Adjutant one pace to right and rear.*)

COMMANDER.—The Chaplain will invoke the Divine blessing. PARADE, *rest!*

CHAPLAIN.—Almighty Father! humbly we bow before Thee, our Creator, Preserver, Guide, and Protector. We thank Thee for our lives; for the mercy which has kept us until this hour; for Thy guidance in our marches by day and by night; for Thy constant care in the hour of danger; and for the preservation of our national integrity and unity. Be graciously near to our comrades who suffer from disease or wounds, and to the widows and orphans of those who fell in our holy cause; in all distress comfort them, and give us willing hearts and ready hands to supply their needs. Grant that the memory of our noble dead, who freely gave their lives for the land they loved, may dwell ever in our hearts. Bless our country; bless our Order; make it an instrument of great good; keep our names on the roll of Thy servants, and at last receive us into that Grand Army above, where Thou, O God, art the Supreme Commander.

COMRADES.—Amen!

COMMANDER.—Attention! Adjutant, you will read the orders for the day.

[The Adjutant will then read the order of the Post Commander, and the National and Department orders for Memorial Day (unless these are to be read in the general services in the cemetery); also order of exercises, details for decoration of graves, etc., etc.]

COMMANDER.—Comrades, the duty of to-day is of impressive significance. We meet to honor our dead

and to deepen our reverence for their worth; to
strengthen among ourselves the bond of fraternity
by recalling the memory of experiences common to
us all; to encourage a more generous charity for
our comrades who are sick or in distress, and for
the destitute wards of the Grand Army; to renew
our pledge of loyalty to our country and our flag,
and to emphasize in the minds and hearts of all
who may unite with us the privilege and duty of
patriotism.

It is expected that throughout our services each
one will manifest the most courteous and reverent
decorum. Let our soldierly deportment be such
that we may worthily honor the graves we decorate, the memories we cherish, the flag we salute,
and the Grand Army to which we belong.

[Should it have been necessary for comrades who
had been detailed at a regular Post meeting for any
special service to perform such duty previous to this
parade, the Commander will call for their report.

Should it be necessary for such details to attend to
the duty assigned them after parade, the Commander
will announce the time and place of re-assembling, and
then order, "Parade dismissed!"

* If the Post is to decorate the graves in a body, the
Commander, after the above address, will order the
Post to move in column by fours to the place where
such decoration is to take place. The music on parade
to and from the graves shall be that of *fife* and *drum*.
If a band is desired, it shall be used only on street
parade *after decoration*, on the way to the hall or grove

---

* See Special Service at Cemetery, page 11.

where the memorial address is to be made, at that place, and on the return to the Post Hall or place of assembly.

When the Post in a body decorates graves, or when, after the decoration of graves by detachments, the Post assembles for service in the cemetery, or when a cenotaph is decorated to the unknown (or unreturned) on some parade-ground, a firing party with three rounds of blank cartridges shall be detailed to do escort duty, who shall march with arms reversed, unloaded; and at the cemetery or cenotaph, or at some other convenient place, after the decoration of graves and cenotaph has been completed, the Commander shall order the officer in charge of the firing party, "Salute the dead!" And that officer shall order, " Recover, arms! Order, arms!" etc., to "Fire!"

The Commander shall then dismiss the parade, or take up the line of march to Post Hall, and then dismiss to such time as further exercises shall be had, unless such exercises proceed immediately.

* These exercises are supposed to be more public in their character.]

---

* See Public Exercises, page 15.

SPECIAL SERVICE AT CEMETERY.

[Should there be this special service, the address of the Commander beginning "Comrades, the duty of to-day is of impressive significance," will not be given until the Post, band or choir, and attendant friends have taken their position about some monument or grave. Then this service shall be used.]

COMMANDER.—"Comrades, the duty of to-day," etc. (See page 8.)

MUSIC.—By band or choir.

CHAPLAIN.—*Let us pray.* Almighty God, in the name of our Lord Jesus Christ, who brought life and immortality to light, we bow before Thee on this Memorial Day. We thank Thee that out from the carnage of war we have come to these days of peace. We thank Thee that the valor, and devotion, and sacrifice unto death of those whose memories we revere vindicate our expectations that no threat against our country's honor shall ever be accomplished; but as in the past thou didst give to our dead the spirit of fidelity and of heroism, so Thou wilt give to those steadfast in the cause of human rights and liberty, of law and order, of social justice and national rectitude, Thy wisdom to direct, Thy might to strengthen, Thy love to bless

O God, teach us to honor our dead by serving the country for which they died. O God, teach us to be grateful to our dead for what they wrought for us by our ready helpfulness of those, the widow and orphan, whose right it is to mourn. O God, teach us to decorate the graves of our dead not only with a tribute beautiful and fragrant, that must fade, but with that fraternity whose love shall endure, with that charity that is fruitful of good works, with that loyalty which, while true to our country's flag, is supremely devoted to the cross, the symbol of our faith.

We thank Thee for peace: that the anger of cannon no longer burdens the air, that the gleam of the sabre and bayonet no longer blinds the eyes, that the passion of war is stilled, and that mercy ministers to those who have submitted to the authority of the nation. May we give them a soldier's pardon, not forgetting the wrong that was done in the charity we accord.

Continue, we pray Thee, the memory of the dead; strengthen, we pray Thee, the hearts of the living; bless, we pray Thee, our whole people, that it may be a nation whose God is the Lord; deepen and ennoble that faith that shall make the Grand Army of the Republic the color-guard of the nation's patriotism, and let our country now and forever be the "land of the free and the home of the brave." And to the end that all for which we pray may be wrought out in us effectually, grant, O God, that by Thy grace we may be enlisted in Thy great army of the redeemed, under Jesus Christ the Captain of our salvation. Amen!

COMMANDER.—To-day is the festival of our dead. We unite to honor the memory of our brave and our beloved, to enrich and ennoble our lives by recalling a public heroism and a private worth that are immortal, to encourage by our solemn service a more zealous and stalwart patriotism. Festival of the dead! Yes, though many eyes are clouded with tears, though many hearts are heavy with regret, though many lives are still desolate because of the father or brother, the husband or lover, who did not come back; though every grave, which a tender reverence or love adorns with flowers, is the shrine of a sorrow whose influence is still potent though its first keen poignancy has been dulled,— despite of all, to-day is a festival, a festival of our dead; no less a festival because it is full of solemnity.

And now, as in this silent camping ground of our dead, with soldierly tenderness and love, we garland these passionless mounds, let us recall those who made their breasts the barricade between our country and its foes. Let us recall their toils, their sufferings, their heroism, their supreme fidelity in camp, in prison-pen, on the battle-field and in hospital, that the flag under which they fought and from the shadows of whose folds they were promoted may never be dishonored; that the country for whose union and supremacy they surrendered life may have the fervent and enthusiastic devotion of every citizen ; that, as we stand by every grave as before an altar, we may pledge our manhood that, so help us God, the memory of our dead shall encourage and strengthen in us all a more loyal patriotism.

OFFICER OF THE DAY (*or comrade to whom the duty has been assigned*).—In your name, my comrades, I scatter (or deposit) these memorial flowers upon this grave (or monument), which represents the graves of all who died in the sacred cause of our country. Our floral tribute shall wither. Let the tender fraternal love for which it stands endure until the touch of death shall chill the warm pulse-beat of our hearts.

CHAPLAIN (*or comrade to whom the duty has been assigned*).—Comrades, by this service, without distinction of race or creed, we renew our pledge to exercise a spirit of fraternity among ourselves, of charity to the destitute wards of the Grand Army, and of loyalty to the authority and union of the United States of America, and to our glorious flag, under whose folds every Union soldier's or sailor's grave is the altar of patriotism.

COMRADES.—Amen !

COMMANDER (*to the officer in charge of the firing party*).—Salute the dead !

OFFICER —Recover, arms ! Order, arms ! etc. Fire !

HYMN.—" My country, 'tis of thee."

BENEDICTION.

PUBLIC EXERCISES.

[This service is meant especially for public halls, although the special service at cemetery could be used, excepting what is said by the Officer of the Day and Chaplain in the act of decoration. The Scripture reading in this service could be introduced into the Special Service at cemetery if no further public exercises are to be had.

The audience is supposed to be seated. The Post enters in uniform, and, covered, file into the space before the seats they are to occupy. The Commander, standing just before the Post, or upon the platform where invited guests, orator, and Chaplain are seated, says:]

COMMANDER.—Attention ! ——— Post, ——, Dept. ————, G. A. R. The Adjutant will read memorial orders from headquarters. (*Aajutant then reads such parts of Orders from Department Headquarters and National Headquarters as may have been previously designated by the Commander.*)

COMMANDER.—Obedience is a soldier's duty. It is not, however, merely in obedience to the order [or orders] read that we assemble here. The most generous instincts of our hearts prompt us to do what the orders from headquarters command. This day commemorates a valor on sea and on land that is illustrious. This day is eloquent with a patriotism which did not speak only from the lips. This day is sacred with the almost visible presence of those who, out of prison-pens and hospitals, from camps and battle-fields, have joined the innumerable company of those who muster to-day upon the parade-ground of heaven. Comrades, SALUTE THE DEAD !

[At this command, every comrade and the Commander will place his left hand upon his heart and raise his hat with his right hand. Standing so for a moment in silence, the Commander, letting his left hand drop to his side, and replacing his hat on his head, will say:]

COMMANDER.—Attention ! (*A brief pause.*) Uncover, (*A brief pause.*) *One rap.*

COMMANDER (*removing his hat after the Post is seated, will say:*)

Friends: As Commander of this Post, I welcome you, in the name of my comrades, to this public service. To us, this is the memorial day of stalwart bravery, of patriotic heroism, of national faith. It is the freedom day of a race emancipated from bondage, and of a nation redeemed from iniquity. It is dear to every soldier. It deepens in our hearts a memory of our brave and our beloved,—the grand army of the immortals; and that memory makes precious to us the badge of the G. A. R., which we wear upon our breasts.

May we join so reverently in these exercises,

that what we call Memorial day may be to our dead their day of coronation.

MUSIC.—By band or choir [such as " Keller's American Hymn"].

COMMANDER.—The significance of this day is not without the indorsement of Holy Scripture. Hear what may well apply to our

G. A. R. AND THE FLAG.

The Lord gave the word : great was the army of those that published it. Ps. lxviii. 11.

Declare ye among the nations, and publish, and set up a standard. Jer. l. 2.

In the name of our God we will set up our banners. Ps. xx. 5.

I cannot hold my peace, because Thou hast heard, O my soul, the sound of the trumpet, the alarm of war. Jer. iv. 19.

COMMANDER.—Senior Vice-Commander, what words of Holy Scripture may refer to the

NAVY?

S. V. C.—They that go down to the sea in ships, that do business in great waters : these all see the works of the Lord, and His wonders in the deep. For He commandeth, and raiseth the stormy wind, which lifteth up the waves thereof. Then they cry unto the Lord in their trouble, and He bringeth them out of their distresses. He maketh the storm a calm, so that the waves thereof are still. Then are they glad because they be quiet ; so He bringeth

them unto their desired haven   Oh, that men
would praise the Lord for His goodness, and for
His wonderful works to the children of men!   Ps.
cvii. 23, 24, 25, 28–32.

COMMANDER.—Junior Vice-Commander, what Scripture
may apply to the

ARMY?

J. V. C.—To your tents, O Israel. So all Israel went
to their tents. 2 Chron. x. 16.   The children of
Israel shall pitch their tents, every man by his own
camp, and every man by his own standard, throughout their hosts. Num. i. 52.   Thou hast given a
banner to them that fear Thee, that it may be dis-
played because of the truth. Ps. lx. 4.   The Lord
shall utter His voice before His army : for His camp
is very great : for he is strong that executeth His
word ; for the day of the Lord is great and very
terrible : and who can abide it ? Joel ii. 11.
Hear, O Israel, ye approach this day unto battle
against your enemies : let not your hearts faint,
fear not, and do not tremble, neither be ye terrified
because of them : for the Lord your God is He that
goeth with you, to fight with you against your enemies, to save you. Deut. xx. 3, 4.   Some trust in
chariots, and some in horses ; but we will remember the name of the Lord our God. Ps. xx. 7.

COMMANDER.—Officer of the Day, if the work of the
navy and army is well done, what proclamation
from Holy Writ can you make?

O. D.—A proclamation of

PEACE.

Lord, Thou wilt ordain peace for us: for Thou also hath wrought all our works in us. Isaiah xxvi. 12.

How beautiful upon the mountains are the feet of him that bringeth good tidings, that publisheth peace; that bringeth good tidings of good, that publisheth salvation; that saith unto Zion, Thy God reigneth! The Lord hath made bare His holy arm in the eyes of all the nations; and all the ends of the earth shall see the salvation of our God. Isaiah lii. 7, 10.

COMMANDER.--Even with such a peace, something remains for us to consider. Chaplain, tell us of

THE NATION AND ITS DEAD.

CHAPLAIN.--Thou hast increased the nation, O Lord, Thou hast increased the nation; Thou art glorified; Thou hast removed it far unto all the ends of the earth. Thy dead men shall live: together with my dead body they shall arise. Awake and sing, ye that dwell in the dust: for thy dew is as the dew of herbs, and the earth shall cast out the dead. Isaiah xxvi. 15, 19.

He will swallow up death in victory; and the Lord God will wipe away tears from off all faces: and the rebuke of His people shall He take away from off all the land; for the Lord hath spoken it. Isaiah xxv. 8. In that day shall this song be sung in the land of Judah: We have a strong city, salvation will God appoint for walls and bulwarks. Isaiah xxvi. 1.

COMMANDER.—And, as an end to all, what is to be our

VICTORY?

CHAPLAIN.—This is the victory that overcometh the world, even our faith. 1 John v. 4. Finally, my brethren, be strong in the Lord and in the power of His might. Put on the whole armor of God, that ye may be able to stand against the wiles of the devil. For we wrestle not against flesh and blood, but against principalities, against powers, against the rulers of the darkness of this world, against spiritual wickedness in high places. Wherefore take unto you the whole armor of God, that ye may be able to withstand in the evil day, and having done all, to stand. Stand, therefore, having your loins girt about with truth, and having on the breast plate of righteousness; and your feet shod with the preparation of the gospel of peace. Above all, taking the shield of faith, wherewith ye shall be able to quench all the fiery darts of the wicked. And take the helmet of salvation, and the sword of the Spirit, which is the word of God. Eph. vi. 10-18.

War a good warfare, holding faith and a good conscience. 1 Tim. i. 18, 19.

Our Saviour Jesus Christ hath abolished death, and hath brought life and immortality to light through the gospel. 2 Tim. i. 10. Thou, therefore, endure hardness as a good soldier of Jesus Christ. 2 Tim. ii. 3.

For this mortal must put on immortality. So when this mortal shall have put on immortality, then shall be brought to pass the saying that is written, Death is swallowed up in victory. O death, where is thy sting? O grave, where is thy victory? The sting of death is sin, and the strength of sin is the law. But thanks be to God, which giveth us the victory through our Lord Jesus Christ. 1 Cor. xv. 53–58.

COMMANDER.—Attention! ——— Post, ——. After such words from Holy Scripture, it is fitting now that we invoke the Divine blessing. PARADE, *rest!*

CHAPLAIN.—" Almighty God, in the name of our Lord Jesus Christ, who brought life and immortality to light," etc. (See page 11.)

COMRADES.—Amen!

COMMANDER.—Attention! (*One rap.*)

MUSIC.—By band or choir.

ADDRESS.—By —— ——.

MUSIC.—By band or choir, closing with the national ode, " America "

COMMANDER.—Chaplain, pronounce the benediction.

CHAPLAIN.—The grace of our Lord and Saviour Jesus Christ, the love of God, and the communion of the Holy Spirit, be with us all. Amen!

COMRADES.—Amen!

[The Post may now be dismissed. It is better, however, after requesting the audience to remain seated, for the Post to take up line of march to Post Hall, or some other convenient place, and there be dismissed.]

DEDICATION

OF ANY

SOLDIERS' AND SAILORS' MEMORIAL.

DEDICATION SERVICES.

[THE Post shall escort the city or town officials and invited guests from some designated place of assembly to the monument or hall where the exercises are to be had. The city or town officials and invited guests are to be seated on the platform. At the front of the platform is an altar, over which is thrown an American flag on which are two swords crossed, the hilts towards the Commander, or president of the day, and on the swords an open Bible. The Post is drawn up in front of the platform, and, if out of doors, as near the memorial as possible.]

MUSIC.—By choir or band.

The mayor, chairman of the selectmen, or the president of the day, in a few words, surrenders the memorial to the Post for dedication.

[For example : Commander ——— Post, ——, Dept. ———, G. A. R.: I have been authorized to invite you at this time to accept from the citizens of ——, at the hands of its accredited representatives, this memorial, and to request that it may be dedicated by you to the noble purpose for which it has been set up (or erected).]

COMMANDER.—*Mr. Mayor [or Chairman of the Board of Selectmen, or President of the Day]* : In the name of my comrades of the Grand Army of the Republic, representing as they do all soldiers and sailors who defended the integrity and authority of the nation, I thank you, and those whom you represent, for this memorial shaft [or statue, or tablet, etc.].

Its very silence is impressive. Without articulate speech, it is eloquent. It needs no words. It is itself an oration. It assures us that our dead are held in remembrance,—those dead who gave their lives for the security of the citizen and the union of the States. It is significant of brave and loyal obedience to the command of the nation always and everywhere, since the obligations of citizenship are not restricted to time or place, or to the conflict of arms. It gives encouragement for the future, since the recognition and approval it gives of patriotic fidelity and heroism will be an incentive for the display of public valor and virtue in all coming time.

There can be no doubt that the honor you pay to the patriot dead, and to their memorable deeds, will serve not only to make American citizenship in these days more reputable, but also to maintain and perpetuate, through all future generations, the union and authority of the United States of America. Adjutant, you will detail a guard of honor.

ADJUTANT (*reads a list of names, each man, as his name is called, answering " Here ! "*).—Commander, the guard is present.

COMMANDER.—Officer of the Day, you will direct the Officer of the Guard to station this detail near [or about] the memorial shaft [statue, tablet, etc.].

COMMANDER.—Holy Scripture saith : The Lord gave the word ; great was the army of those that published it. Ps. lxviii. 11.

Declare ye among the nations, and publish, and set up a standard. Jer. l. 2.

In the name of our God we will set up our banners. Ps. xx. 5.

Officer of the Day, you will order the guard of honor to raise [or display] our flag.

OFFICER OF THE DAY.—Officer of the Guard, let the flag be raised [or displayed].

MUSIC.—Band or choir, "Star Spangled Banner."

COMMANDER.—The forces of the nation are divided into two great arms, that of the navy and that of the army. Senior Vice-Commander, what words of Holy Scripture may apply to the

NAVY?

S. V. C.—They that go down to the sea in ships, that do business in great waters: these see all the works of the Lord, and His wonders in the deep. For He commandeth, and raiseth the stormy wind, which lifteth up the waves thereof. Then they cry unto the Lord in their trouble, and He bringeth them out of their distresses. He maketh the storm a calm, so that the waves thereof are still. Then are they glad because they be quiet; so He bringeth them unto their desired haven. Oh, that men would praise the Lord for His goodness, and for His wonderful works to the children of men. Ps. cvii. 23, 24, 25, 28–32.

COMMANDER.—Officer of the Day, let the guard of honor set up the symbol of the navy, and let a sailor be detailed to guard it.

[An anchor is then set up against the shaft, crossed
with a cutlass or boarding-pike. A comrade, dressed
as a sailor, stands guard with drawn cutlass.]

COMMANDER.—Junior Vice-Commander, what Scripture
    may apply to the

ARMY?

J. V. C.—To your tents, O Israel So all Israel went
to their tents. 2 Chron. x. 16. The children of
Israel shall pitch their tents, every man by his own
camp, and every man by his own standard, throughout their hosts. Num. i. 52. Thou hast given a
banner to them that fear Thee, that it may be dis-
played because of the truth. Ps. lx. 4. The Lord
shall utter His voice before His army; for His
camp is very great; for he is strong that executeth
His word; for the day of the Lord is great and
very terrible: and who can abide it? Joel ii. 11.
Some trust in chariots, and some in horses; but we
will remember the name of the Lord our God.
Ps. xx. 7.

COMMANDER.—Officer of the Day, let the guard of
    honor set up the symbol of the army, and let a
    soldier be detailed to guard it.

[A musket with fixed bayonet, canteen and haversack
hanging from it, knapsack leaning against the stock, is
set up against the shaft opposite to the anchor. A comrade in full soldier uniform, armed with a musket with
fixed bayonet, stands guard.]

COMMANDER.—Officer of the Day, if the work of the
    navy and army be well done, what proclamation
    from Holy Scripture can you make?

OFFICER OF THE DAY.—A proclamation of peace.

Lord, Thou wilt ordain peace for us : for Thou also hath wrought all our works in us. Isaiah xxvi. 12. How beautiful upon the mountains are the feet of him that bringeth good tidings, that publisheth peace ; that bringeth good tidings of good ; that publisheth salvation ; that sayeth unto Zion, Thy God reigneth! The Lord hath made bare His holy arm in the eyes of all the nations ; and all the ends of the earth shall see the salvation of our God. Isaiah lii. 7, 10.

COMMANDER.—The Chaplain will now offer the prayer of dedication.

CHAPLAIN.—Almighty God, we thank Thee for Thy sovereign care and protection, in that Thou didst lead us in the days that were shadowed with trouble, and gavest us strength when the burden was heavy upon us, and gavest us courage and guidance, so that after the conflict we have come to these days of peace. We thank Thee that the 'wrath of war has been stilled, that brother no longer strives against brother, that once again we have one country and one flag.

May Thy blessing be upon us as a people, that we may be Thy people, true and righteous in all our ways, tender and patient in our charity, though resolute for the right ; careful more for the downtrodden than for ourselves, eager to forward the interests of every citizen throughout the land, so that our country may be indeed one country from the rivers to the seas, from the mountains to the plains

We pray Thee to make our memories steadfast, that we may never forget the generous sacrifices made for our country. May our dead be enshrined in our hearts. May their graves be the altars of our grateful and reverential patriotism.

And now, O God, bless Thou this memorial!

Bless it, O God, in honor of mothers who bade their sons do brave deeds:

In honor of wives who wept for husbands who should never come back again:

In honor of children whose heritage is their fallen fathers' heroic name:

In honor of men and women who ministered to the hurt and the dying:

But chiefly, O God, in honor of men who counted not their lives dear when their country needed them; of those alike who sleep beside the dust of their kindred or under the salt sea, or in nameless graves, where only Thine angels stand sentinels till the reveille of the resurrection morning. Protect it and let it endure, and unto the latest generation may its influence be for the education of the citizen, for the honor of civil life, for the advancement of the nation, for the blessing of humanity, and for the furtherance of Thy holy kingdom.

Hear us, O our God; we ask it in the name of Him who made proof of the dignity and who consecrated the power of sacrifice in His blessed life and death, even in the name of Jesus Christ, the great captain of our salvation. Amen!

COMRADES.—Amen!

COMMANDER.—Attention ! ——— Post, ——, Dept. ———, G. A. R. In the name of the Grand Army of the Republic, I now dedicate this memorial shaft [or statue, or tablet, etc.]. I dedicate it to the memory of those who in the navy [*the sailor on guard will salute*] guarded our inland seas and ocean coasts, and fell in defence of the flag. I dedicate it to the memory of those who in the army [*the soldier on guard will salute*] fought for our hillsides and valleys and plains, and fell in defence of the flag. I dedicate it to the memory of those who on land and on sea fought for the Union, and fell in defence of the flag [*the guard of honor will salute and stand at salute*]; who on land and on sea fought for the authority of the Constitution, and fell in defence of the flag; who on land and on sea fought for their country, and fell in defence of the flag. Comrades, salute the dead !

[Each comrade who is armed will present arms; those not armed will place the left hand open, fingers outstretched, over the left breast, and with the right hand raise the hat or cap four inches above the head.]

COMMANDER (*after a brief pause*).—Attention ! *In place.* REST.

COMMANDER.—Mr. Mayor, our service of dedication is ended. In the name of my comrades I thank you, and those you represent, for your courtesy in permitting us, who are bound by special ties to them, to honor our dead.

[The Mayor may then make a few remarks, or indicate to the band or choir that there will be music.]

ADDRESS.

MUSIC.

MAYOR.—Commander, our exercises are ended.

COMMANDER.—Attention! —— Post, ——, Dept. ——, G. A. R. As we close these services, the guard of honor is withdrawn, the symbols of the army and navy are removed, the flag is lowered; but the memorial we have dedicated remains, guarded by our dead. So long as it shall endure, it shall speak to us and to all of the loyalty and heroism in the army and navy, and of that significant national authority of which our flag is the symbol to every true American heart.

Officer of the Day, remove the symbols. (*After a pause.*) Lower the flag. (*After a pause.*) Dismiss the guard.

Chaplain, pronounce the benediction.

CHAPLAIN.—The grace of our Lord and Saviour Jesus Christ, the love of God, and the communion of the Holy Spirit, be with us all. Amen!

COMRADES.—Amen!

[The Commander will then, if necessary, escort the city or town officials and invited guests to Post Hall or other suitable place, and then dismiss parade, or dismiss the parade immediately at the close of the exercises.

The special circumstances of the occasion will suggest what is best to be done; preserving, so far as possible, a soldierly method.]

THE BURIAL OF THE DEAD.

BURIAL OF THE DEAD.

I. A Post may attend funerals of deceased comrades, or of soldiers and sailors honorably discharged from the army or navy, when a request shall have been made by the deceased or his family or friends, upon order of the Commander or vote of the Post.

II. The Post shall assemble at residence of deceased comrade, or at the place where religious services are to be held, and the Commander shall detail a sufficient number of comrades as pall-bearers, if so requested.

III. The remains shall then be escorted to the grave or to limits of town or city, or otherwise as circumstances may dictate, in the order as laid down in Army Regulations: left in front, the Post preceding the hearse, and a guard of honor surrounding the remains.

IV. The Officer of the Day shall, under the Commander, take charge of the pall-bearers and guard of honor.

V. Arriving at the grave, the Post shall halt, open order, and allow the remains to pass to the front, when they shall be placed upon the bier.

VI. The Post shall then be formed about the grave or tomb in most fitting manner appropriate to the occasion and the nature of the ground.

VII. The last offices of respect due to the defenders of the Republic shall then be paid according to the following

RITUAL.

COMMANDER takes position at head of coffin.
CHAPLAIN takes position at foot of coffin.
OFFICERS and PAST COMMANDERS in rear of Commander.
POST in rear of Chaplain.
COLORS to front.

1. COMMANDER.—Assembled to pay our last tribute of respect to this dead soldier (or sailor) of our Republic, let us unite in prayer. The Chaplain will invoke the Divine blessing.

2. PRAYER BY CHAPLAIN.—God of battles! Father of all! amid these monuments of the dead we seek Thee with whom there is no death. Open every eye to behold Him who changed the night of death into morning. In the depths of our hearts we would hear the celestial word, "I am the Resurrection and the Life; he that believeth in Me, though he were dead, yet shall he live." As comrade after comrade departs, and we march on with ranks broken, help us to be faithful unto Thee and to each other. We beseech Thee, look in mercy on the widows and children of deceased comrades, and with Thine own tenderness console and comfort those bereaved by this event which calls us here. Give them "the oil of joy for mourning, the garment of praise for the spirit of heaviness." Heavenly Father! bless and save our country with the freedom and peace of righteousness, and, through Thy great mercy, a Saviour's grace, and Thy holy Spirit's favor, may we all meet at last in joy before

Thy throne in heaven. And to Thy great name shall be praise for ever and ever !

ALL COMRADES.—Amen !

[3. If a choir be present, an appropriate hymn will now be sung.]

[4. The Commander may then speak as follows, or, if he elects, extemporize :]

COMMANDER.—One by one, as the years roll on, we are called together to fulfil these last sad duties of respect to our comrades of the war. The present, full of the cares and pleasures of civil life, fades away, and we look back to the time when, shoulder to shoulder on bloody battle-fields, or around the guns of our men-of-war, we fought for our dear old flag. We may indulge the hope that the spirit with which, on land and sea, hardship, privation, dangers were encountered by our dead heroes—a spirit un-complaining, nobly, manfully obedient to the behest of duty, whereby to-day our Northern homes are secure and our loved ones rest in peace under the ægis of the flag—will prove a glorious incentive to the youth who, in the ages to come, may be called to uphold the destinies of our coun-try. As the years roll on we, too, shall have fought our battles through and be laid to rest, our souls following the long column to the realms above, as grim death, hour by hour, shall mark its victim. Let us so live that when that time shall come those we leave behind may say above our graves, "Here lies the body of a true-hearted, brave, and earnest defender of the Republic."

FIRST COMRADE (*laying a wreath of evergreen or flowers upon the coffin*).—In behalf of the Post, I give this tribute, a symbol of an undying love for comrades of the war.

SECOND COMRADE (*laying a rose or flower upon the coffin*). —Symbol of purity, we offer at this lowly grave a rose. May future generations emulate the unselfish devotion of even the lowliest of our heroes.

THIRD COMRADE (*laying a laurel leaf upon the coffin*).— Last token of affection from comrades in arms, we crown these remains with a symbol of victory.

[Then the Chaplain shall repeat the following, or make an address of about the same length :]

CHAPLAIN'S ADDRESS.—The march of another comrade is over, and he lies down after it in the house appointed for all the living. Thus summoned, this open grave reminds us of the frailty of human life and the tenure by which we hold our own. "In such an hour as ye think not, the Son of man cometh."

It seems well we should leave our comrade to rest where over him will bend the arching sky, as it did in great love when he pitched his tent, or lay down, weary and footsore, by the way or on the battle-field for an hour's sleep. [As we leave our comrade to rest, no longer to hear the sound of the waves, or to float upon the bosom of the deep, no longer to sail beneath peaceful skies, or to be driven before the angry storm, may he find welcome in that land where there is no more sea.*] As he was then, so he is still,—in the hands of the Heavenly Father. "God giveth His beloved sleep."

As we lay our Comrade down to rest, let us cherish his virtues and learn to imitate them. Reminded forcibly, by the vacant place so lately filled by him, that our ranks are thinning, let each one be so loyal to every virtue, so true to every friendship, so faithful in our remaining marches, that we shall be ready to fall out to take our places at the great review hereafter, not with doubt, but in faith that the merciful Captain of our salvation will call us to that fraternity which, on earth and in heaven, remains unbroken. (*A pause for a moment.*) Jesus saith, "Thy brother shall rise again. I am the Resurrection and the Life." (*The body is deposited in the grave or tomb.*) Behold, the silver cord is loosed, the golden bowl is broken: we commit the body to the grave, where dust shall return to the earth, and the spirit to God who gave it. Earth to earth, ashes to ashes, dust to dust, looking for the resurrection and the life to come through our Lord Jesus Christ.

PRAYER.

---

* I suggest that the words enclosed in brackets be used at the burial of a sailor.—J. F. LOVERING, *C.-in-Chief.*

NOTE.—The foregoing service was adopted by the National Encampment at New Haven, Conn., May 14 and 15, 1873.

THE MEMORIAL SERVICE.

A MEMORIAL SERVICE,

TO BE USED IN THE

POSTS OF THE GRAND ARMY OF THE REPUBLIC,

IN

Grateful and Devout Commemoration of Deceased Comrades.

Memorial Service.

[The Post will open without ceremony, the officers in uniform, and sentinels properly stationed; the friends and relatives of the deceased, present by invitation, seated in the body of the hall. The altar will be covered with the national flag, draped black and white, and ornamented with flowers. A chair (or chairs, according to the number of deceased comrades), suitably draped, will be placed between the Post Commander's chair and the altar. The person appointed to deliver the address will be seated on the right of the Commander. A comrade will be detailed as drummer.

The exercises will begin with a VOLUNTARY or CHANT, and proceed as follows:]

POST COMMANDER.—Adjutant, for what purpose is this meeting called?

ADJUTANT.—To pay our tribute of respect to the memory of our late comrade [or comrades] ————.

POST COMMANDER.—Have you a record of his [their] service in the cause of our country, and in the Grand Army of the Republic?

ADJUTANT.—Commander, I have.

POST COMMANDER.—You will read it.

ADJUTANT.— ———— was born [here give date] in the town of ————, State of ———— ; enlisted in Co. ———— Reg't ———— Volunteers, on the ———— day of ————, 186 ; held the office [or offices] of ————, and was discharged ————, 186 . He joined ———— Post, No. ————, Department of ———— ; held the office [or offices] of ————, and died ———— , aged ——— years.

[The drummer will beat three rolls upon a muffled drum immediately after the reading of each record.]

POST COMMANDER.—The record is an honorable one, and as the memory of all faithful soldiers of the Republic should be cherished, and their record preserved, I direct that it be placed in the archives of the Post for future reference.

[The exercises will continue with a RESPONSIVE SERVICE by the Chaplain of the Post and the comrades and friends present, or the choir, as may be thought best.]

CHAPLAIN.—"What man is that liveth and shall not see death? Shall he deliver his soul from the hand of the grave? If a man die, shall he live again?"

COMRADES [or choir].—"Jesus Christ said, 'I am the Resurrection and the Life. He that believeth in Me, though he were dead, yet shall he live. And he that liveth and believeth in Me shall never die.'"

CHAPLAIN.—"Let not your heart be troubled. Believe in God; believe also in Me. In My father's house are many mansions. I go to prepare a place for you."

COMRADES.—"Blessed are the dead who die in the Lord. Yea, saith the Spirit, that they may rest from their labors."

CHAPLAIN.—"They shall hunger no more, neither thirst any more."

COMRADES.—"Neither shall the sun light on them, nor any heat."

CHAPLAIN.—"For the Lamb which is in the midst of the throne shall feed them and lead them unto living fountains of water."

COMRADES.—"And God shall wipe away all tears from their eyes."

CHAPLAIN.—"There shall be no more death, neither sorrow, nor crying; neither shall there be any more pain."

COMRADES.—"For the former things have passed away."

[Then shall follow a hymn or chant by the choir. The comrades shall then form a square, enclosing the altar, the officers in front, the Chaplain at the altar.]

PRAYER.—By the Chaplain, closing with the Lord's Prayer in concert.

CHANT.—By the choir.

[The comrades will return to their places.]

READING of a brief selection of Scripture from the Ninetieth Psalm or the fifteenth chapter of the First Epistle to the Corinthians.

HYMN.

ADDRESS.

DOXOLOGY.

[After which the Post shall be closed as follows :]

POST COMMANDER.—Senior Vice - Commander, how should all men live?

SENIOR VICE-COMMANDER.—With trust in God, and in love for one another.

POST COMMANDER.—Junior Vice - Commander, how should comrades of the Grand Army live?

JUNIOR VICE-COMMANDER.—Having on the whole armor of God, that they may be· able to withstand in the evil day.

POST COMMANDER.—The last enemy that shall be destroyed is death.

COMRADES.—We thank God, who give thus the victory through Jesus Christ our Lord.

POST COMMANDER.—May the Almighty God, our Heavenly Father, keep us by His gracious presence amid the conflicts of our mortal life, and at last receive us into everlasting peace.

COMRADES.—Amen!

POST COMMANDER.—I now declare this Post closed.

NOTE.—The foregoing service was prepared by the committee appointed by Par. 4, G. O. No. 4, Series of 1874, and approved by Par. 1, G. O. No. 7, Series of 1874.

INSTALLATION OF OFFICERS.

INSTALLATION CEREMONIES.

[THE Department Commander shall detail a comrade to act as his representative in the installation of officers of Posts, who shall be designated for the time being as MUSTERING OFFICER.

In cases where an officer is elected to fill a vacancy, he shall be installed by the P. C., unless the vacancy filled is that of P. C., when the senior P. P. C. will act.

Should the M. O., from any cause, fail to be present at the time for installation, the senior P. P. C. will act as M. O.

The M. O. will report at the encampment of the Post, passing the O. G. with the national countersign, and announce to the I. G. his name, rank in the Grand Army of the Republic, and the purpose of his visit.

The I G. will call, " Officer of the Guard, the Mustering Officer ! "

The O. G. will retire, receive from the M. O. the order detailing him, and report to the P. C., who will then address the Post.]

P. C.—Comrades, Comrade A —— B—— is now present for the purpose of installing the officers of this Post. You will receive him with proper honors, and pay the strictest attention during the ceremonies. Officer of the Day, you will retire to the anteroom and introduce the Mustering Officer.

[The O D. having retired, the P. C. will call up the Post, when the officers shall take position one pace in advance of their respective stations and draw sabres. The O. D. and M. O. will pass to the centre of the room, facing the P. C., and halt.]

O. D.—Commander, I have the honor to introduce Comrade A ———— B ————, who has been detailed to install the newly-elected officers of this Post.

P. C.—Post, PRESENT, *arms!*

[Comrades will salute by raising the right hand to visor of cap; sentinels within the camp will present arms, and officers will salute with sabres.

The M. O. will return the salute, and comrades will, at the order of the P. C., resume position of "Attention!" and sentinels "Carry, arms!"]

P. C.—Comrade, as the representative of our Department Commander, and as a comrade of the Grand Army of the Republic, we extend to you a soldiers' welcome. I have the honor to turn over to you the command of this Post. We are ready to obey your instructions.

[The M. O. will then take the position of the P. C., the P. C. stepping to the right.] (*One rap.*)

M. O.—Comrades, the purpose of my visit having been already made known to you, we will at once proceed with our duties.

Post Commander, Adjutant, and Quartermaster, you will present yourselves before the altar. (*They do so.*)

Comrades, the Rules and Regulations require the Adjutant and Quartermaster to make out the reports of the Post, and present the same to the Post

Commander, to be forwarded to Department Headquarters. Adjutant and Quartermaster, have you
each performed this duty?

A. AND Q. M.—We have.

M. O.—Post Commander, have these reports, with the
per capita tax, been duly forwarded?

P. C.—They have.

[Should the officers be unable to answer these questions
affirmatively, the M. O. will require the reports to be
made before proceeding further.]

M. O.—Commander, has the bond of the Quartermaster
been duly executed and delivered to you as required
by the Rules and Regulations?

[Unless answered affirmatively, the M. O. will decline
to install the Q. M.
The P. C., Adjt., and Q. M. will then resume their
stations.]

M. O.—The Adjutant will announce the officers elect.
(*The Adjutant does so.*)

[NOTE.—Should any of the retiring officers be among
those to be installed, they will vacate their stations,
which shall be filled by temporary details.]

M. O.—Officer of the Day, present for installation the
Senior and Junior Vice-Commanders, Surgeon,
Quartermaster, Officer of the Day, and Officer of
the Guard.

[The officers will be placed, in order of rank, in front
of the altar.]

M. O.—Comrades, you have been designated by the suffrages of your comrades to fill the various offices of this Post. It is important that the duties of your positions should be promptly and intelligently discharged, and I therefore call your attention to Art. VIII., Chap. II., Rules and Regulations. (*The M. O. will read the following sections :*)

SECT. 2. The Vice Post Commanders shall perform such duties as are required of them by the Ritual, and in the absence of the Commander shall take his place in the order of their rank. If neither of them are present, the Post shall elect a Commander *pro tempore*.

SECT. 4. The Quartermaster shall hold the funds, securities, vouchers, and other property of the Post, and fill all requisitions drawn by the Adjutant and approved by the Post Commander; he shall collect all moneys due the Post, giving his receipt therefor; he shall keep an account with each member, and notify all comrades in arrears; he shall render a monthly account in writing to the Post of its finances, which shall be referred to an auditing committee appointed by the Post. He shall make and deliver to the Post Commander all reports and returns required of Post Quartermasters by Chap. V., Art. II., and shall deliver to his successor in office, or to any one designated by the Post, all moneys, books, and other property of the Post in his possession, or under his control. He shall give security for the faithful discharge of his duties as provided in Chap. V., Art. VII.

SECT. 5. The Surgeon shall discharge such duties in connection with his office as may be required of him.

(*And also to* Art. II., Chap. VII.)

SECT. 4. The Quartermaster of each Post shall, through the Post Commander, make a quarterly return to the Assistant Quartermaster-General of the Department on the first days of January, April, July, and October, on blanks of Form B.

You are also expected to perform such other duties as may be required of you by the Ritual, the By-Laws of this Post, and the constituted authorities of the Grand Army of the Republic. Are you ready to assume these duties? .

OFFICERS.—We are.

M. O.—You will each raise your right hand and repeat after me the obligation of office:

I (A——— B ———), on my word of honor as a man and as a comrade of the Grand Army of the Republic, do solemnly pledge myself to perform faithfully and impartially all the duties of the office upon which I am about to enter. SO HELP ME GOD!

M. O.—Officer of the Day, conduct these comrades to their respective stations:

[The O. D. will conduct the officers separately to their stations, commencing with the lowest in rank. The retiring officers will rise, salute, invest their successors with the insignia of office, and then turn over to them all property of the Post in their possession.]

M. O.—Officer of the Day, present for installation the Chaplain elect.

M. O. — Comrade, you have been selected by your comrades to conduct the religious exercises of this Post. The Rules and Regulations of the Grand Army of the Republic also require you to officiate at the funerals of comrades, when attended by the Post, and to perform such other duties in connection with your office as the Post may direct. Are you willing to assume and perform the duties of this office in a reverent spirit?

CHAPLAIN.—I am.

M. O.—Comrade, it is expected that you will so dignify your office that your example may be followed by all your comrades, and that there may be no reproach cast on the religion whose precepts it is your duty to recite for our counsel and guidance.

M. O.—The Officer of the Day will conduct the Chaplain to his station.

M. O.—The Post Commander elect will now present himself for installation.

[The P. C. will appear before the altar.]

Comrade, the fact that you have been elected by the comrades of this Post to the responsible office of Commander indicates that they have satisfactory confidence in your ability and integrity, and that they feel assured that you will strictly and impartially discharge all the duties incumbent upon you.

They confide the welfare of this Post to your keeping; any breach of this trust will act injuriously upon the Grand Army, and bring discredit upon every comrade. Let their confidence, therefore, be fully justified by your fidelity. You are, by virtue of your position, a member of the Department Encampment, and it is expected that you will attend its meetings, and exhibit an interest generally in the necessary work of perfecting and maintaining our organization. Realizing fully these responsibilities, are you willing to take the obligation of your office?

P. C.—I am.

M. O.—Raise your right hand toward heaven, and repeat after me the obligation of your office:

I (A—— B———), having been elected Commander of —— Post, No. ——, Department of ——, Grand Army of the Republic, on my word of honor as a man and a comrade of the Grand Army of the Republic, do most solemnly pledge myself to faithfully and impartially perform, in letter and spirit, all the duties incumbent upon the office upon which I am about to enter. I promise to obey the lawful orders of my superior officers, and to exact the obedience of others thereto, and to the full extent of my abilities and opportunities to advance the interest of this Post and of the Grand Army of the Republic.

Should this Post disband during my term of office, or before the installation of my successor, I solemnly promise to close up its affairs honorably, and to forward all the property of the Department, including charter, rituals, books of record, and Post papers, to Department Headquarters, as required by the Rules and Regulations. So help me God!

M. O.—Comrade, you will now announce the name of your Adjutant.

P. C.—I announce Comrade ———— as Adjutant.

M. O.—Comrade ————— will present himself before the altar.

[The Adjutant takes position at the left of the Post Commander.]

M. O.—Comrade, in accordance with the Rules and Regulations, the Commander has appointed you Adjutant of this Post. As he depends greatly upon you for the proper management of the affairs of the Post, for which he is responsible to the Department Headquarters, this appointment proves that he places great confidence in your ability. Your duties, as recited by Sect. 3, Art. VIII., Chapter II., Rules and Regulations, are manifold and laborious.

[Reads Sect. 3, Art. VIII., Chap. II., Rules and Regulations.]

If your work be done in an imperfect manner, it will greatly retard the progress of this Post. If, however, you give proper thought and attention to your duties, you will materially aid the organization and be of great service to the Post Commander; and you are expected to use every opportunity to prove yourself worthy the honor bestowed on you.

Raise your right hand, and repeat after me the obligation of your office:

I (A———— B————), on my word of honor as a man and a comrade of the Grand Army of the

Republic, do solemnly pledge myself to perform strictly and promptly all the duties incumbent upon me as Adjutant. So HELP ME GOD!

M. O.—The Adjutant will nominate his Sergeant-Major.

ADJUTANT.—I nominate A—— B——.

M. O.—The Quartermaster will nominate his Quartermaster Sergeant.

Q M.—I nominate C—— D——.

M O.—Post Commander, do you confirm these nominations?

P. C.—I do.

M. O.—Comrades A—— B—— and C——— D—— will present themselves before the altar.

M. O.—Comrades you are to assist the Adjutant and Quartermaster, respectively, in the discharge of their duties. You will raise your right hand, and repeat after me the obligation of your office:

I (A—— B——, and C—— D——), on my word of honor as a man and a comrade of the Grand Army of the Republic, do solemnly pledge myself to perform faithfully and impartially all the duties of the office upon which I am about to enter. So HELP ME GOD! (*Two raps, calling up the officers.*)

M. O.— Comrades, in accordance with the requirements of our Order, I have performed my duty in thus installing you into your respective offices. It remains for you to prove whether this night's work has been a good one. It is expected that each will at once make himself entirely familiar with his

duties, whether specifically prescribed or not, and
become thoroughly acquainted with the Rules and
Regulations of the Grand Army of the Republic,
the Ritual, the By-Laws of the Post, and the Orders
from National and Department Headquarters.
Exercise a spirit of fraternal confidence and good
fellowship, and be ready to extend a helping hand
to every comrade when opportunity offers.   Be
true to yourselves and to the Order, and this Post
will prosper.   (*Three raps.*)

Comrades of the Post, I now present to you the
officers of your choice.   I counsel you to aid them
in the performance of their duties ; to strengthen
their hands, and to encourage them in their labors.
With your help their term of office may be highly
successful ; without it, the result of their labors
must be barren.

I invoke all to cherish the principle of *Fraternity ;*
let there be no cold reserve in your intercourse ; let
the disparity of rank or position necessary for
active service be laid aside here, and each one re-
gard all others as comrades.   Inculcate a spirit of
true charity.   Seek out and aid the deserving poor,
who would rather starve than press their necessities
upon you.   Let them know that the help the
soldier gives to his crippled comrade, or to the
widows and orphans of the fallen, is not the alms-
giving that parades itself for the commendation of
the world, but a pure and holy offering, tendered
in the spirit of our holy religion,—the practical
exemplification of the Golden·Rule.   Finally, com-

rades, having proven your *Loyalty* to our country, be loyal to each other. If your comrade is worthy of your friendship, stand by him though the whole world assail him.

Let us cherish and strengthen a feeling of dependence and confidence in each other, and show to the world that we are worthy of having served our country in the Grand Army of the Republic.

[The Post Commander will now take his position, the M. O. stepping to the right for this purpose, handing the gavel to the P. C.; O. D. and A., S. M. and Q. M. S. taking their respective stations.

If the M. O. wishes then to retire, he will advance to the centre of the room, and there be joined by the Officer of the Day.]

P. C.—Comrade, you will accept the thanks of this Post and its officers for the manner in which you have discharged your duties. It will give us pleasure at all times to have you visit us. Bear with you our fraternal wishes for your own welfare, and report to the Department officers that we shall do all in our power to advance the interests of the Grand Army of the Republic. Post, PRESENT, *arms!*

[Post will give the usual salute. When the M. O. has retired past the I. G., the order will be given, "Carry, arms!"] (*One rap.*)

NOTE.—Adopted in accordance with General Order No. 13, Series of 1871, from National Headquarters.

FORM OF INSPECTION.

National Headquarters, G. A. R., }
Philadelphia, Feb. 28, 1884. }

The following Form of Inspection has been prepared in accordance with the action of the National Encampment at Denver, and all officers and comrades are required to observe the same.

By command of Robert B. Beath,
Commander-in-Chief
Jno. M. Vanderslice,
Adjutant General.

FORM OF INSPECTION.

—

ON occasion of a regular inspection of a Post the following form will be used : —

The Inspecting Officer, having previous to the opening of the Post notified the Post Commander of his intention to inspect the Post, will, upon the calling of the Post to order, take his seat in the body of the Post room, the better to observe the opening ceremony and the working of the Post.

The regular order of business, as provided in the Ritual, will be attended to, and after muster, if any, or if none be had on the night of inspection, then, when the order of business has reached the portion '' New Business,'' the Inspecting Officer will proceed to the rear of altar, salute, and retire to the ante room.

The P. C. will then rise and announce to the Post that by Special (or General) Order, No. —— from headquarters, Comrade ——— will now proceed to inspect this Post, and caution the comrades that during the ceremony strict attention should be given ; he will then proceed to explain the form that will be used during the inspection. When the Commander has concluded these remarks, he will demand : '' Adjutant, are your books and papers in form for inspection, orders properly filed, and papers in order ? ''

The P. C. will then demand : ·· Quartermaster, are your books all posted, and vouchers properly filed, and ready for inspection ? "

The P. C will then inquire in like manner: " Officer of the Guard, are the arms and accoutrements prepared for inspection ? " (*Answer.*)

Upon receiving answers to these inquiries the P. C. will say : " The Officer of the Day will act as escort to the Inspecting Officer."

The Inside Sentinel will then give one rap on the door to indicate readiness, whereupon the Inspecting Officer will rap for admittance. The Sentinel, upon opening the door, will demand, " Who goes there ? " The Inspecting Officer will announce his name and position. (*At the same time giving Department coun tersign to the Sentinel.*)

The Sentinel will announce : " Officer of the Guard ! Comrade ——— Assistant (or Dept.) Inspector."

The O. G. will salute the P. C., and announce that the Inspecting Officer is in waiting.

The P. C. will say : " Officer of the Day, you will proceed to the outpost, and escort the Inspecting Officer."

The O. D. will advance to rear of altar, salute, and proceed to the inner door, and command, "Sentinel, you will admit the Inspecting Officer."

(*Three Raps.*)

The O. D. will then escort the Inspecting Officer to rear of altar.

The O. D. will then say : " Commander, I have the

pleasure to introduce Comrade —— Assistant (or Department) Inspector."

The P. C. will order " Present Arms !" to which the Inspecting Officer will reply by saluting.

The P. C. will then order, " Carry Arms!" and say: " Comrade, the Post is ready for inspection, and we await your orders."

Then I. O. will request the Commander to seat the Comrades, which done, he will proceed to the Adjutant's desk, inspect the books and orders, see that the orders are correctly filed, and ascertain if any are missing. After procuring such information as he desires from the Adjutant, he will, (under escort of the O. D.) proceed to the Q. M. desk (passing in rear of altar and saluting.) and ascertain from the Q. M. the financial standing of the Post, the amount expended for charity during the year, the number of Comrades in good standing, and those suspended, after which the I. O. will receive from the Post Commander the answers to the inquiries as required on Form H.

The I. O. will then announce (*saluting Commander.*): " The inspection is closed ; with your permission I will now retire," and proceeds to rear of the altar, facing P. C.

The P. C. will now call up the Post: " Present Arms!" The I. O. will acknowledge salute, and retire.

The P. C. will then seat the Comrades, and proceed with the regular order of business.

THE END.